A Let's-Read-and-Find-Out Book™
Revised Edition

THE BEGINNING OF THE EARTH

by Franklyn M. Branley   illustrated by Giulio Maestro

A Harper Trophy Book
Harper & Row, Publishers

LET'S READ-AND-FIND-OUT BOOK CLUB EDITION

The *Let's-Read-and-Find-Out Science Book* series was originated by Dr. Franklyn M. Branley, Astronomer Emeritus and former Chairman of the American Museum–Hayden Planetarium, and was formerly coedited by him and Dr. Roma Gans, Professor Emeritus of Childhood Education, Teachers College, Columbia University.

Let's-Read-and-Find-Out Science Book is a registered trademark of Harper & Row, Publishers, Inc.

The Beginning of the Earth
Text copyright © 1972, 1988 by Franklyn M. Branley
Illustrations copyright © 1972, 1988 by Giulio Maestro
10 9 8 7 6 5 4 3 2 1
Revised Edition

Library of Congress Cataloging-in-Publication Data
Branley, Franklyn Mansfield, 1915–
    The beginning of the earth.

    (Let's-read-and-find-out science book)
    Summary: Describes what may have happened when the Earth began billions of years ago.
    1. Earth—Juvenile literature. [1. Earth]
I. Maestro, Giulio, ill. II. Title. III. Series.
QB631.B69 1988   525.1   87-47765
ISBN 0-690-04676-6
ISBN 0-690-04654-5 (lib. bdg.)

    "A Harper trophy book."
ISBN 0-06-445074-0 (pbk.)   87-45677

Title page photo courtesy of NASA (Apollo 17 mission), provided by SCIENCE GRAPHICS, Bend, Oregon.

Earth has not been here forever. Neither have the sun or moon, Mercury or Mars, or any of the other planets. Long ago they did not exist.

No one knows exactly where they came from. No one knows exactly how they were formed, or when it all happened, either. But people have ideas about such things.

We know that Earth is a planet and that there are other planets in the solar system. We know that Earth is only one small part of the solar system and that the sun is the biggest part of all.

People believe that the sun and all the planets formed in the same way, from the same materials, and at about the same time. So the story of the beginning of the Earth is also the story of the beginning of the sun and the whole solar system.

Before there were the sun and the planets, there was
nothing but a big cloud of dust and gases. That was
about ten billion years ago—much longer ago than
anyone can really understand. The cloud was
huge—much larger than the whole solar system is today.

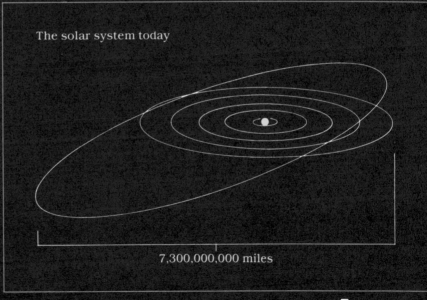

The solar system today

7,300,000,000 miles

The bits of gas and dust moved about, colliding with one another. Once in a while two or more bits of material stuck together; they made a clump. Gradually each clump gathered in more material. The clumps grew larger. The smooth gas cloud became lumpy, like a cake with raisins in it.

Many of the clumps joined together. They collected more
and more dust and gases, so they grew bigger and bigger.

One clump grew larger than all the others. Nearly all
the dust and gases collected to make that one large
clump. It was to become the sun, the main part of the
solar system. That was about five billion years ago.

Leftover dust and gases formed smaller clumps. About four and a half billion years ago, nine of these smaller clumps became the planets.

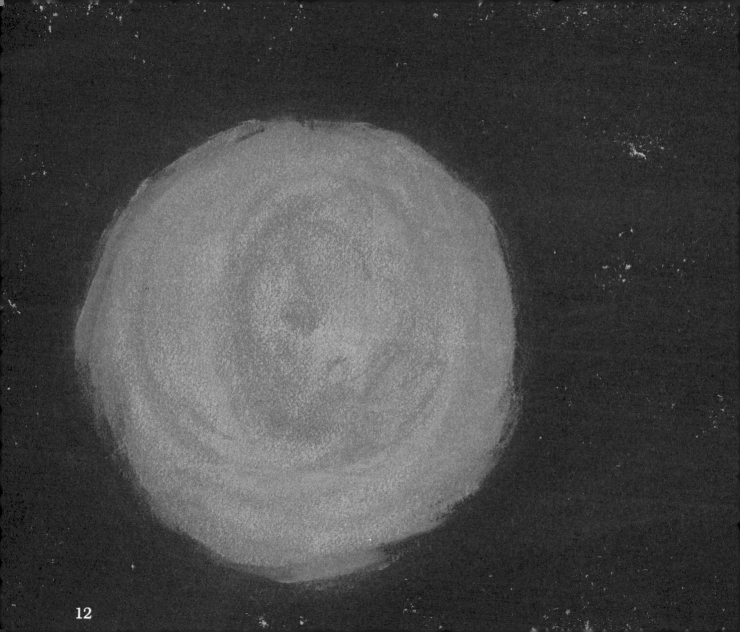

12

One of these smaller clumps was the Earth-clump. The Earth-clump pulled in more and more material. The material packed together tighter and tighter. The clump became hotter and hotter, though not nearly as hot as the sun. The sun was much larger, and it was much, much hotter.

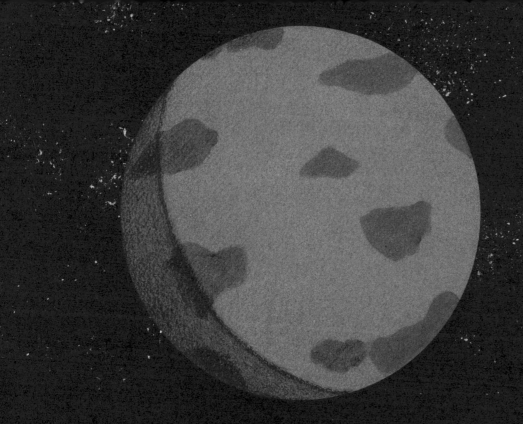

After a long time, the new Earth began to cool. Oxygen, iron, copper, silicon, and many other materials that were in the dust cloud joined together to make minerals—the minerals that rocks are made of.

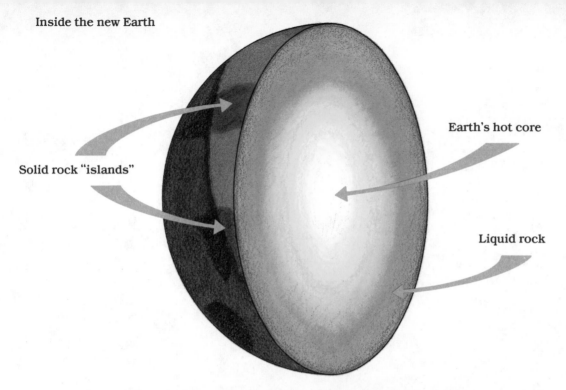

Earth's hot core

Solid rock "islands"

Liquid rock

At first the rocks were not solid like the rocks we see today. They were melted, or molten. Earth was so hot that after millions of years the rocks were still molten.

In time some of the outer parts of the new Earth cooled and became solid. There were islands of solid rock in a sea of liquid rock.

Many people believe that around this time a huge chunk of rock, dust, and gases, perhaps as big as Mars, crashed into Earth. The chunk broke apart. So did part of the Earth. Bits and pieces of both of them flew into space. Some of these pieces formed into a ring around the new planet. Gradually the bits and pieces joined together, to make the moon.

The new Earth, now smaller than it had been, was covered by dark clouds. No sunlight could get through.

Water fell from the clouds. Lightning flashed among the clouds. The rain did not reach the surface of the Earth. Earth was so hot, the rain changed to water vapor as it fell, and went back into the clouds.

As the years went by, Earth continued to cool. The rock islands grew bigger. For thousands of years the rain kept falling. It came closer and closer to the surface before it changed back to water vapor.

At some time, the rain finally reached parts of Earth's surface. But Earth was still so hot, the rain boiled and steamed. Hot pools of water formed in low parts of the rock islands.

Still the rains came down.

Steam

The outside of Earth cooled slowly. The inside stayed very hot. It still is.

The rock islands and the sea of hot liquid rock were bathed in darkness. No sunshine came through the heavy clouds.

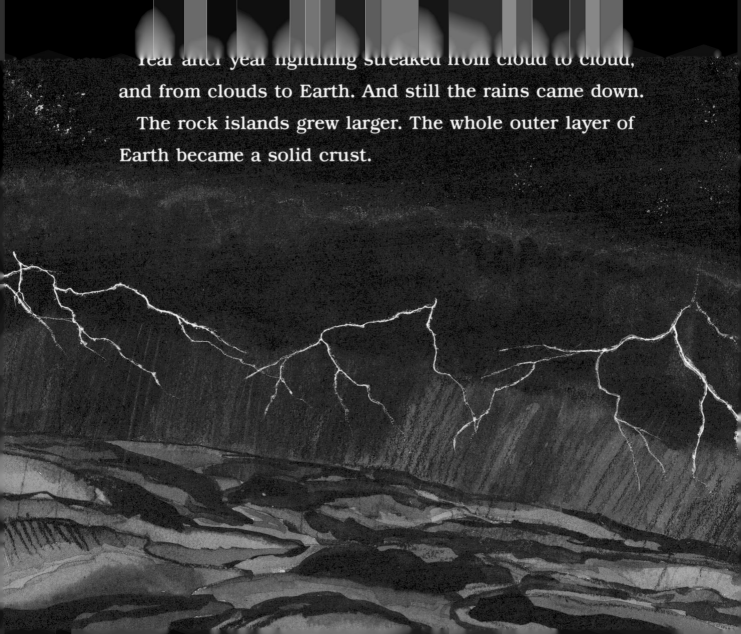

Year after year lightning streaked from cloud to cloud, and from clouds to Earth. And still the rains came down. The rock islands grew larger. The whole outer layer of Earth became a solid crust.

Hot, molten rock broke through cracks. Volcanoes formed all around the new Earth. They shot gas, dust, ash, water, and chunks of rock into the dark clouds. Hot, molten rock—lava—spouted out of the volcanoes. It spread over the solid crust and hardened.

Parts of Earth heaved upward and became mountains. The cones of volcanoes cooled. They too became mountains.

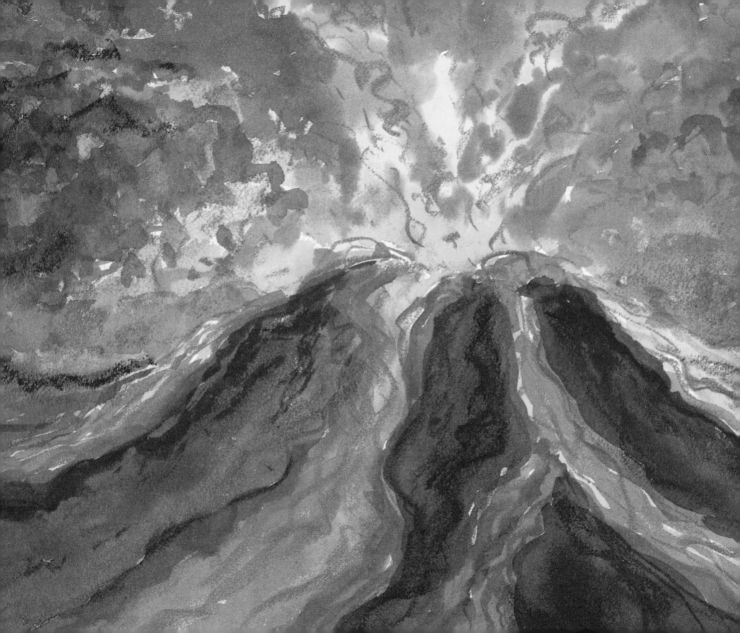

Other parts of the crust sank, to become basins. Hot water flowed into them as it rained overhead.

The basins overflowed. All over the Earth, water filled low places. Lakes formed, and lakes grew into oceans.

There came a time when the rains stopped, the heavy dark clouds became thinner, and the sun burst through.

The new Earth was a dead, lifeless world. But the skies were clearing, and Earth was bathed in sunshine.

Then, out of the young Earth and the water that covered a large part of it, life began. This happened more than three billion years ago.

But that is another story.

Earth kept changing.

The solid crust that here and there poked above the oceans broke into giant chunks. They moved on the molten rock beneath.

About 250 million years ago

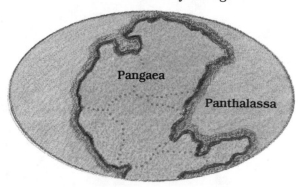

After millions of years the chunks of rock moved together, to make one gigantic land mass. We call it Pangaea (pan-JEE-uh), which means "all the land."

Pangaea was surrounded by water that reached around the world. The water we call Panthalassa (pan-thuh-LASS-uh), which means "all the water, or seas."

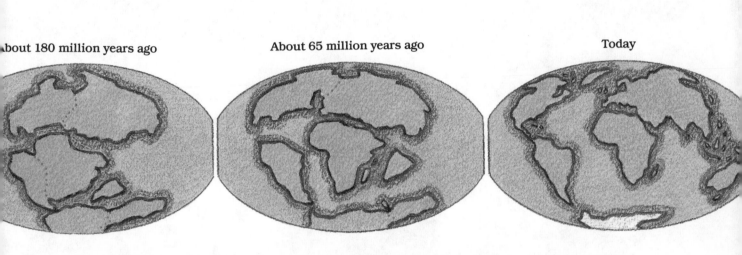

About 180 million years ago   About 65 million years ago   Today

After millions of years Pangaea broke apart, to become
the continents that we know today.

And so we think the sun and Earth and all the other planets came from a huge cloud of dust and gases.

But where did the cloud come from?

We have no final answer to that question. People must learn a lot more about this Earth of ours before it can be answered. We must also learn a lot more about the sun and the stars, and about the whole big universe, of which our planet is only one very small part.

Our solar system